Where Is Easter Island?

by Megan Stine

illustrated by John Hinderliter

Penguin Workshop
An Imprint of Penguin Random House

For Bill, who thinks he looks like the statues—MS

For Brynn and Dawson, who love puzzles, coloring, and superheroes. Thanks for the smiles—JH

PENGUIN WORKSHOP
Penguin Young Readers Group
An Imprint of Penguin Random House LLC

Library of Congress Cataloging-in-Publication Data is available.

ISBN 9780515159486 (paperback)   10 9 8 7 6 5 4 3
ISBN 9780515159509 (library binding)   10 9 8 7 6 5 4 3 2 1

Contents

Where Is Easter Island?

It was Easter Sunday in April 1722. Jacob Roggeveen had been sailing for more than eight months. He was the commander of three Dutch ships. They were searching the South

Jacob Roggeveen

Pacific for parts of the world that had never been seen or explored. Roggeveen hoped to find a huge, legendary continent that many believed existed. It was called Terra Australis. Other explorers had searched parts of the South Pacific, but no one had found it yet, or mapped the area correctly.

That Easter Sunday, Roggeveen and his crew were a thousand miles from anywhere. Suddenly, they spotted land. What could it be? There was smoke rising in the distance, which meant people lived there. But what kind of people?

Some of the natives in the Pacific islands were peaceful and friendly. But others were not. Jacob Roggeveen had heard stories about cannibals! No one knew how his crew would be greeted by the islanders. Roggeveen decided it was better to wait until morning before he and his men went ashore. He named the island Paasch Eyland—the Dutch words for Easter Island—since that's the day he had arrived.

The next morning, the weather was rainy— not the best time to put small boats into the water. And besides, his men were nervous. Maybe they should wait another day.

But natives on the island had seen the Dutch ships offshore and were eager to find out who these strange visitors were. So one of the island people got into a canoe. He paddled out to Roggeveen's ship and climbed aboard. He was totally naked! He was also friendly and warmhearted.

He danced and
sang with the sailors.
They played a violin for him
and gave him small gifts, including a
mirror and a pair of scissors. The man seemed so
happy, he didn't want to leave. They had to force
him into his canoe to make him go back to the
island. He motioned for them to follow.

It was several more days before the Dutch would finally set foot on the island. When they did, they found something amazing—something no one had ever seen or imagined.

Lining the beach were giant stone statues, as tall as three-story buildings. Some were twenty or thirty feet tall. Others were just huge heads, buried in the sand up to their necks.

How did the statues get there? Who carved them? The islanders had no modern tools. They had no carts with wheels. They lived in simple grass-covered huts. How could they possibly have

carved these huge blocks of stone? How could they have moved such heavy pieces of stone at all?

Roggeveen saw only a few of the statues. He didn't know there were more than nine hundred of them! They were scattered all over the island.

How they really got there, and why, is just part of the story—and the mystery—of Easter Island.

CHAPTER 1
Stranded on a Remote Island

Easter Island is in the middle of nowhere. If you look at a map of the world, the island is so tiny, it's barely even a dot. Lost in the middle of the South Pacific Ocean, it's more than two thousand miles west of South America. The nearest islands are the Pitcairn Islands—more than a thousand miles away. Easter Island is so far away from anywhere else, it's hard to imagine how the earliest people ever found it.

So how did human beings discover the most remote island on earth?

No one is certain, but it is believed that about four thousand years ago, the people who lived in Taiwan began to spread out. They were searching for new places to live. Over many

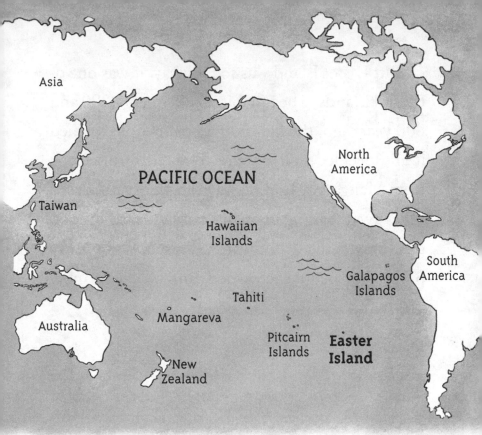

hundreds of years, they sailed from place to place throughout Southeast Asia. They took food and supplies with them and planted crops when they arrived. They formed new colonies on many of the islands in the South Pacific. Those islands are now called Polynesian islands. Hawaii, Tahiti, and New Zealand were also colonized this way.

But Easter Island was so far away, it was one of the last islands to be inhabited. Between 1,200 and 800 years ago, the first Polynesian people reached it and decided to live there. They probably came from Mangareva—an island more than a thousand miles away. Sailing in open double-hulled canoes, they braved the ocean waters. As many as twenty or thirty people crowded into each canoe.

They brought with them chickens, bananas, sugar cane, and taro—a sweet root vegetable like a sweet potato.

The Polynesian people were excellent sailors. They knew how to use the stars to guide them and the ocean currents and winds to sail fast. Still, the trip to Easter Island took at least three weeks—maybe longer. When they finally found the island, they gave it a name, Te Pito o te Henua, which meant "the navel of the world" or "the end of the world." Years later, they named the island Rapa Nui. Rapa Nui means "greater extremity" or "land's end"—as in the end of the land—the farthest thing from anything else. The people who live on the island are called the Rapa Nui people, and the language they speak has the same name.

When the Polynesians arrived, they brought with them their customs and beliefs. They didn't believe in gods. Instead, they thought that their ancestors—family members who had lived before them—had special divine powers. They believed that those ancestors could keep them safe, make food grow, and keep them healthy. They carved wooden statues of their ancestors and put them on stone altars. They didn't worship them like gods, but they did perform special ceremonies to show their respect. Their living leaders were always the descendants—the sons—of these ancestors.

Kon-Tiki

In 1947, the Norwegian explorer Thor Heyerdahl decided to cross the Pacific Ocean on a raft. He thought maybe Easter Island had been settled by people from South America—not people from other Polynesian islands. He wanted to prove that South Americans of that time had the ability to cross the ocean.

To prove he was right, he would try to sail a simple raft from South America to the Polynesian islands. The daring journey was more than five thousand miles long! No one thought he could do it. Thor made a raft out of logs and other plants. He used only the same materials that people could have used eight hundred years ago. The raft was called *Kon-Tiki*—named for the sun god from an ancient South American culture. Thor and five men set sail from Peru. They kept going for 101 days until they hit land five thousand miles away. They hadn't reached Easter Island—they had passed it! Thor filmed the whole trip and made it into a documentary. The 1950 movie was called *Kon-Tiki*. It won an Academy Award.

Was Thor Heyerdahl right? No. Most scientists still believe that Easter Island was settled by Polynesian people, not South Americans. They know because they have tested the DNA of the Easter Island people. It was more similar to the DNA of Polynesian people than to that of South Americans. Those tests weren't available when Thor made his voyage.

The island the first settlers discovered was covered in huge palm trees, at least ninety feet tall. It looked like a paradise. There was plenty of shade from the hot sun. The trees created a rain forest, too. Rain was important for drinking water, and to make the crops grow.

There was food for the first Polynesian settlers, too. They found millions of birds on the islands and hundreds of fish in the sea. Until the first crops grew, they ate fish, birds, dolphins, and birds' eggs. Some of the birds were so tame, they would land on the islanders' heads. For a while, the island must have been a lovely place to live.

But it wouldn't be a paradise forever.

Within four hundred years, nearly all the trees on the island were gone. Without trees, the islanders had no firewood. They couldn't build new canoes or grass huts. The sun beat down on the land, drying it out. Crops wouldn't grow, because there wasn't enough rain. The birds disappeared, too. It was hard to catch fish without canoes. Without new canoes, they couldn't even leave!

The islanders were stranded.

What had turned this beautiful place into a parched, dry, miserable island? The answer was something the islanders may have brought with them when they sailed to Easter Island.

Rats!

CHAPTER 2
Rats!

No one is sure how rats arrived on Easter Island. Maybe a few rats washed ashore on ocean currents. Maybe they surfed the ocean waves on a piece of driftwood, and accidentally landed there. Or very possibly the Polynesian people brought rats along in their canoes on purpose—as a source of food!

No matter how it happened, the Polynesian rats turned out to be very bad for Easter Island. Rats have babies at an incredible rate. The Polynesian rats' numbers could have doubled every forty-seven days. So even if only two rats arrived with the settlers, there could have been millions of them a few years later. Their population exploded because there were no predators on the island to eat the rats.

The problem with rats was that they ate things the island people needed. They ate birds' eggs.  They ate seeds from native plants and from the crops the islanders planted. But most importantly, they ate the nuts that dropped from the huge palm trees.

Those nuts were like acorns. They were the seeds that could make a new tree grow. When the rats ate all the seeds, new trees couldn't sprout up from the ground.

Over time, the forests on Easter Island disappeared. The islanders were also partly to blame. They cut down too many trees, to use for firewood and to make new canoes. They also

used a farming method called "slash and burn."
The ashes from the burned trees made the soil
richer, so crops could grow better. But the soil
only stayed rich for a short time. The islanders
didn't realize that new trees wouldn't grow back
where the older trees had been.

Once the trees were gone, the plentiful rain disappeared. So did the streams and small lakes. So the islanders had to come up with new ways to grow crops. They invented some very smart farming methods.

One of their clever tricks was to build a small circular wall of rocks. It was called a *manavai*. Inside the manavai, they planted crops. When it finally rained, the wall of rocks kept the rainwater in place—sort of like a tiny pool. The rock wall also protected the plants from wind, so they didn't dry out.

Another farming trick was to cover a field with rocks, a practice called lithic mulching. The rocks kept the soil moist. Whenever it rained, tiny amounts of minerals were washed from the rocks into the soil.

Easter Island is sixty-three square miles in area—a little smaller than Brooklyn, New York. When the islanders began farming, they covered nearly half the island with rock gardens! Miles and miles of rocks! More than a billion rocks were used.

It must have taken a lot of cooperation and hard work for the islanders to dig up or break up all those rocks and then put them in place. A lot of cooperation was needed just to live on an island with so little shelter or food.

But the Easter Island people were extremely good at working together. And they were extremely good at working with rocks. They had to be. How else could they have carved so many huge statues in their spare time—and hauled them halfway across the island?

CHAPTER 3
Giant Heads

The huge statues on Easter Island sit on grassy hillsides, overlooking the sea. Or they stand on huge stone bases, lined up in rows like giant soldiers with their backs to the water—a parade of mammoth kings. Some of them wear huge red stone "hats" or crowns, sometimes thought to

be topknots. The hats alone are eight feet high. Other statues are buried in the ground at an angle. Only their enormous heads stick up—as if they grew there all by themselves.

It's one thing to see a huge statue in front of a church or museum in a city. But it's another thing to see hundreds of statues surrounded by nothing but grass, sand, and sea.

How did the statues get there? The statues were enormous. Some of them weighed fifty, sixty, seventy, or eighty tons!

The mystery of Easter Island has puzzled people for years. Some people actually thought ancient aliens might have brought the statues from outer space! Or that space aliens told the islanders how to carve them.

In 1914, the truth about the statues began to come out when Katherine Routledge visited Easter Island. Katherine was a British scientist who studied anthropology and archaeology.  Anthropologists are people who learn how human beings live together, by talking to people and finding out their history. Archaeologists study objects from the past in order to learn about the people and cultures that made them. They dig in the ground to find bits and

Katherine Routledge

pieces of tools or weapons that people once used.

Katherine had a ship built and sailed from England to Easter Island to find out as much as she could about the people who lived there. The ship was named *Mana. Mana* is a Polynesian word that means something like *good luck—*

but it's more than that. It's the word for the supernatural powers that the Polynesian people thought their ancestors had—powers that kept the islanders safe.

Katherine Routledge's ship

Mana and Tapu

In the past, *mana* and *tapu* were two of the most important ideas in the Polynesian world. Polynesian people believed that strong leaders had mana—supernatural powers or strengths. In fact, anything with power was said to have mana. The guns that Europeans carried had mana. So did the huge ships they arrived in.

They also believed that mana could flow into other people if the tapu was good. Tapu was the Polynesian word for the idea of respecting other people and controlling one's own behavior. There were tapu rules to be followed. If a Polynesian person did something bad, it would hurt the tapu. Then they had to perform a ceremony to try to make the tapu right again.

Katherine had heard about the statues from other Europeans who had visited the island. But no one knew how or when or why the statues had been carved. And by the time she arrived on the island, all the statues had fallen. They were toppled over—lying faceup or facedown. Many of them were broken.

There were only about 250 people living on Easter Island when Katherine arrived. She didn't speak Rapa Nui, the language of Easter Island. Luckily, though, one islander was a man named Juan Tepano. He had learned to speak some English. So Juan translated for her, helping her understand what the islanders were saying.

According to the Easter Islanders, the statues had been carved by their ancestors. They were carved at a quarry. A quarry is an area where the earth is solid rock or stone. The quarry on Easter Island was a cliff wall, the side of a volcano crater.

Volcanic Islands

Islands are often formed when a volcano erupts under the sea. Hot lava shoots up from inside the earth's crust. Then it hardens. At first, the lava might form a small mountain underwater. When enough lava rises above the water level, it becomes an island.

Easter Island was formed this way. There were three main volcanoes that created the island. They are all extinct now—they don't erupt. But the lava from them hardened into different kinds of stone: basalt and tuff. Tuff is a softer stone, easy to carve. Most of the statues on Easter Island were carved from tuff, taken from the side of an extinct volcano.

The statues were made to honor the island's leaders and earlier ancestors. Then they were placed on stone altars. The islanders didn't worship them like gods, but they did perform special ceremonies to show their respect. Each statue may have been carved to represent a chief who had led his people in earlier times.

Katherine wanted to find out how the statues were moved across the island. The islanders said the chiefs had so much mana, they simply ordered the statues to walk! They said that the statues walked a little bit each day, until they reached their final resting places.

This answer seemed impossible. However, many years later, islanders showed some visitors how the statues could walk, tilting from side to side—almost like a giant windup toy.

The statues were called *moai* in the language of Easter Island. The stone platforms they stood on were called *ahu*. The ahu were like outdoor altars—places for people to come together to show thanks to the powerful ancestors who kept them safe. There were more than three hundred ahu on the island, most of them near the coast. Some of the ahu were immense—one was more than seven hundred feet long.

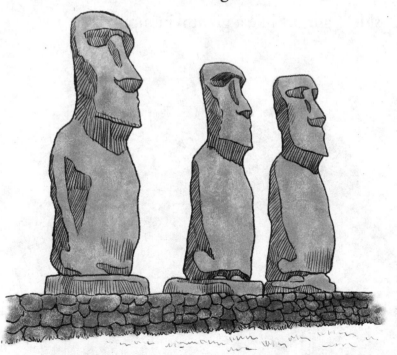

As time went on, Katherine learned more about the customs and beliefs of the people of Easter Island. The chiefs wore feather headdresses. It seemed that hats were a sign of power or strength. That could explain why some of the moai wore huge red hats made of stone.

In the past, the people of Easter Island didn't live all together in villages. Family groups were scattered over the island. In some ways, each group was like a separate tribe, with leaders or chiefs. Some tribes were called "long ears" and some were called "short ears." They didn't mix with each other very much. Each family group carved its own moai and worshipped at an ahu nearby. When times were good, and food was plentiful, about three thousand people lived on the island.

To carve the statues, the islanders made tools from basalt—the hard form of lava from a volcano. It was perfect for making sharp tools that could be used to chisel rock.

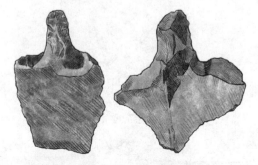

Groups of strong young men would go to the quarry and begin to carve a huge figure right out of the side of the wall of rock. They carved the face first, then the arms and body. Once the front of the statue was carved, they would begin to chip

away at the sides and back. Little by little, they removed enough stone so that the whole statue was only attached to the quarry wall by a thin line down its back. Before chipping away at the final bit of stone, they tied ropes to the statue. The ropes helped them hold on to it and lower it to the ground when they carved it free from the quarry wall.

With the statue standing freely on the ground, the islanders could work on carving the back. The back was just as important as the front. It had to be a certain shape so it would be balanced. They also added decorations to the back—carved pictures.

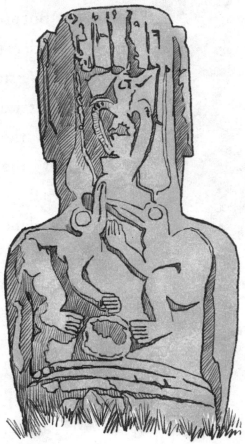

Once the statue was finished and put in place, the eyes were added. The eyeballs were made of

white coral, with shiny black stones in the middle as pupils.

But how did the islanders move the heavy statues to places miles away from the quarry? Did the statues actually *walk* as the islanders said?

In a way, the answer was yes!

Moai with restored eyes

CHAPTER 4
Walking Statues

For years, scientists have been trying to solve the mystery of how the islanders moved more than nine hundred statues across the island without using machines. They had no horses, oxen, or donkeys to help with the heavy work. And the islanders didn't know how to use simple machines, like pulleys. They didn't even have wheels or carts.

So it seemed there were only two possible answers to the mystery. Either the statues were laid flat, and then dragged somehow across the island. Or they were moved upright, in a standing position. Walking!

At first, scientists thought the statues had been moved lying down. It would be hard work, but possible. The islanders could have cut down many trees and used the logs as rollers. They would need to line the way with the logs so they could push the statue onto a rolling path. Or they might have made a sled out of logs. The statue could have been laid on the sled, and the sled dragged by many people.

But the statues were up to thirty-three feet tall, and weighed up to eighty tons! That's more than ten elephants. Would it really be possible for men—even a huge number of them—to drag that much weight?

Thor Heyerdahl thought so. He was the Norwegian explorer and scientist who had sailed on the *Kon-Tiki* raft. In 1955, he went to Easter Island to set up an experiment. He asked 180 islanders to put one of the statues on a sled and drag it with ropes.

Thor Heyerdahl

44

It was only a medium-size statue, not one of the biggest. Still, the islanders struggled with it. Even with so many men working, it was hard to move the heavy stone. So it seemed that Thor was wrong.

After that, other scientists began to think differently. Maybe the Easter Island people were telling the truth. Maybe the statues had "walked"—in a way.

An engineer named Pavel Pavel decided to try a different experiment. He made a concrete

Pavel Pavel

model of a statue. It was fourteen feet tall and weighed twelve tons. Pavel tied long ropes around the statue—some at the head and some at the base. Two teams of eight men each held the ropes. Pavel shouted out commands, telling the men how to pull the ropes to rock the statue from side to side.

It worked! As one team of men jerked their rope, the statue tilted on edge. At the same time, the second group pulled the statue in a twisting motion, to move it forward one step. With Pavel shouting out commands, they soon learned how to make the concrete statue walk forward.

This was called the "refrigerator method." It was similar to the way a man might try to move

a heavy refrigerator all by himself—by tilting it
from side to side, inching it forward.

Thor Heyerdahl heard about Pavel's success.
He asked Pavel to come to Easter Island with him.
In 1986, they duplicated the same experiment,
but with real moai—real statues. It was scary at
first. The men were afraid they might pull too
hard. The giant statue might fall over and crush
them, or break!

But Pavel said that wouldn't happen. Why not? Because the islanders who had carved the statues were very smart. They had deliberately carved them to be well-balanced. The statues had a low center of gravity, which meant that it was hard to knock them down. Like a bowling pin that's tapped on the side, they could rock back and forth and not fall over. It would take a lot of force to make a statue fall.

It only took eight people to move a small nine-foot moai. Then they tried it again with a larger statue. It was twelve feet tall. Sixteen people were able to make it walk easily.

Pavel said the ancient islanders could probably move the statues up to six hundred feet each day. It would take about nine days to move one statue a mile, as long as the road was smooth and flat. Some statues were near the quarry and had to be moved only a short distance—less than a mile.

But others had been walked as much as six or seven miles from where they were carved.

Thor Heyerdahl was amazed when he saw the statues walking. He said it looked like walking "a dog on a leash."

The Easter Islanders were not surprised. For years and years they had been told that the statues walked. They even had a song about the walking statues. And they had a special word for it, too: *neke-neke.* The word meant "walking without legs."

Not everyone agreed that the statues "walked" to their destinations this way. Other scientists noticed ancient paths or roads on Easter Island. These grass-covered paths led from the quarry to the different statue sites. Each path was lined on both sides with rocks—like curbs. Did these paths mean that the statues were pushed or pulled on large sleds after all?

Probably not. However, the roads *were* used to transport the statues. We know because the paths are littered with fallen statues—statues that toppled over as they were being moved. Even though the statues were designed to be stable, they could tip over on hills. If they were going downhill, they fell on their faces. If they were going uphill, they fell backward, onto their backs.

Since all the fallen statues on the roads were facing away from the quarry, it meant they were on their way to somewhere else. Once they fell, they were probably too heavy for the islanders to

lift up again. Besides, they were broken. So the islanders just left them there, lying along the roads.

No scientist has come up with a better explanation for how the statues were moved. The easiest, simplest, fastest way to move them was with two or three ropes and a group of about fifteen men. In 2012, a scientist named Terry Hunt made a copy of a statue. Then he made a video showing how the statue walked. You can see it on YouTube. Check the bibliography on page 108 to get the video link.

Still, there was one remaining mystery about Easter Island. Why were all the statues toppled over by the time Katherine Routledge arrived?

What had happened? Not all of them fell

while they were being moved. Many had been knocked off their platforms—on purpose—and had broken. It was clear that they had been toppled over in an angry fit—or as an act of war.

What happened to change everything for the islanders? What terrible event came and stole the way of life they had always known and loved?

CHAPTER 5
Dangerous Visitors

To Jacob Roggeveen and the Dutch sailors who first reached Easter Island, the islanders seemed so strange. They were mostly naked, with tattoos all over their bodies. Many of them had objects in their earlobes. Their earlobes hung down almost to their shoulders.

They spoke a language that the Dutch couldn't understand. The Dutch were a little bit afraid of them.

But as it turned out, the native people were friendly and trusting. It was the Dutch who did harm to the islanders, not the other way around.

On that first day, the islander had come to meet their ship. But the Dutch were still afraid to go ashore. So the next day, more islanders swam out to meet them. They came in rafts or paddled small canoes. They didn't wait to be invited. They scrambled aboard the Dutch ships, bringing presents—roasted chickens and bananas.

Roggeveen's men were grateful for the food. They had been at sea for a long time. The fresh fruit was a treat.

However, the sailors were surprised by what happened next. Smiling and friendly, the natives began to take things. They snatched hats off the sailors' heads! They picked the sailors' pockets, and grabbed every loose piece of wood they could find. Then they jumped overboard and swam to shore.

The same thing happened again the following day. The natives seemed to be especially fond of hats. And they didn't seem to think it was wrong to take other people's things. They stole as many hats and caps as they could grab. They didn't realize the sailors needed hats aboard ship to protect them from the hot sun.

When Roggeveen decided to go ashore with his men they brought their muskets with them, and split up into several groups. Some of the sailors stayed near the shore to guard their five sloops. Sloops were the small boats they had rowed to shore in. Roggeveen went inland.

All of a sudden, Roggeveen heard a gunshot. He hurried back to find out what happened. It turned out that one of his sailors had panicked. Afraid of the grabby islanders, the sailor had fired his gun. Then others did, too. In the end, nine or ten islanders were dead—including the good-natured man who had danced with them on their very first day.

Roggeveen and his crew felt terrible. They blamed their one fearful crew member for all the deaths. No one wanted to hurt the islanders. They sailed away as soon as they could, feeling sorry, but as if they had left the islanders "as good friends."

But the islanders were changed forever after that visit. They were terrified by the guns. They had never seen such powerful weapons before. It changed how they thought about one another, about their ancestors, and the world.

Weapons weren't the only kind of misery that

Europeans brought to Easter Island. Within just a few years, many islanders would be dead from something they had no way to protect themselves against—disease.

CHAPTER 6
Disease

The Dutch didn't mean to bring sickness and death to the Easter Islanders. But they came in close contact with the islanders, spreading germs. And the islanders were so friendly and sweet-

natured. They liked to dance with the Dutch sailors and share food with them. Some of the women kept kissing the sailors.

The problem was that the Easter Islanders had never been exposed to the diseases that were common in Europe—smallpox, measles, flu, syphilis, and tuberculosis. They didn't have any immunity. Immunity is the ability to fight off germs that cause diseases. As time went on, when the islanders got the new diseases, they died in large numbers.

Smallpox Blankets in America

Native Americans suffered the same fate— illness and death—when Europeans first arrived in America. The native people had never been exposed to smallpox, measles, or flu. They had never even caught the common colds that the British brought with them. The diseases killed them off quickly since they had no immunity.

Shortly after the French and Indian War, a British officer decided to use disease as a way to fight the Indians. He gave the Indians two blankets and a handkerchief from a smallpox hospital. He *wanted* the Native Americans to get smallpox! The commanders hoped the blankets would spread disease to others in the tribe. No one knows whether this terrible trick worked. But even without the blankets, smallpox and other diseases wiped out more than half the population of Native Americans by the end of the nineteenth century.

In 1770, more visitors from Europe arrived on Easter Island. This time it was Spanish explorers, arriving from Spanish-owned Peru in South America. The Spanish played music for the islanders. Then they traded with them, sharing all their germs as well as their European habits. They kissed the island women. The problem with disease happened all over again.

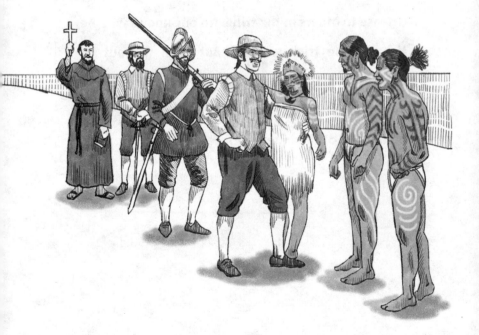

At first, the islanders were impressed and amazed by the Spanish. The Spanish knew how to write! They showed the island chiefs a piece of paper. The islanders had never seen written words before. Then the Spanish showed the chiefs how to "sign" the paper by making marks with ink. The paper was a contract or agreement. As far as the Spanish were concerned, they had just bought Easter Island for Spain!

The islanders didn't know they had sold their island. They were so in awe of Europeans, they wanted to copy everything they did. They thought the Europeans were gods. They measured the Europeans' ships with lengths of string. They were probably amazed by such big boats. Boats were important on Easter Island. The islanders even built their houses in the shape of an upside-down boat. They hoped that the shape would bring mana to their families. The stone foundations of the boat-shaped houses are still visible on Easter Island today.

A boat-shaped house

After the Spanish visit, the islanders invented their own form of writing. They wanted to be more like the powerful Spanish men who had guns, hats, and big ships. They called their own writing *rongorongo*. It didn't have letters, just pictures. But using the new writing made the island chiefs seem more powerful to everyone else.

Soon after the Spanish visit, though, hundreds of islanders became sick from diseases they had never known. Then they began to fight among themselves. With hundreds of people dying, the islanders may have wondered: Were their ancestors still protecting them?

By the time a British explorer named Captain James Cook arrived in 1774, the huge statues were no longer standing.

The islanders were friendly to Captain Cook. They brought bananas out to his ship, which filled the crew with joy. Bananas! The sailors hadn't seen fresh fruit in a long time.

But there wasn't much else to eat on the island—only a few sweet potatoes and very few chickens.

The crew traded with the native people and drank from the fresh water—probably spreading more of their germs. Cook's men spent five days on the island. The people were warm and welcoming, but they were sickly. It was clear that the islanders had seen better times.

By the time he left, Captain Cook understood that something terrible had happened to the people on Easter Island. But he had no idea that he and other Europeans just like him were to blame. He didn't realize that it was disease from Europe that had already changed the islanders' way of life forever.

In the years before Cook arrived, wars had broken out among the Polynesian people who had previously been so peaceful. During the wars, most of the statues were knocked down.

MOUNT PUI

VOLCANO PUAKATIKE

VOLCANO RANU RARAKU

AHU TONGARIKI

CENTRAL AMERICA

SOUTH AMERICA

EASTER ISLAND

A row of moai statues facing inland at Ahu Tongariki

Restored moai statues at Ahu Akivi

Rano Kau volcanic crater

Moai statues

No one knows for sure why the Polynesians did it. Maybe they pulled down their enemies' statues, as an act of war. Or maybe they pulled down their own statues, because so many islanders were dying of disease that they no longer trusted their ancestors to have mana that would keep them safe.

But war and disease weren't the only problems the islanders faced. More visitors would soon arrive, bringing another kind of misery to Easter Island.

Who Was Captain Cook?

Captain Cook

Captain Cook was one of the most famous explorers of his time. He was the first European to sail to Hawaii. Like Roggeveen, he was searching for Terra Australis—a huge southern continent at the "bottom" of the world near Antarctica. He finally realized it didn't exist. But he did find the small continent of Australia as well as New Zealand. (Australia was named after the legendary Terra Australis.) He mapped their coastlines and also mapped many of the islands in the South Pacific. A group of islands near New Zealand is named for him—the Cook Islands.

On his first visit to Hawaii, the native people

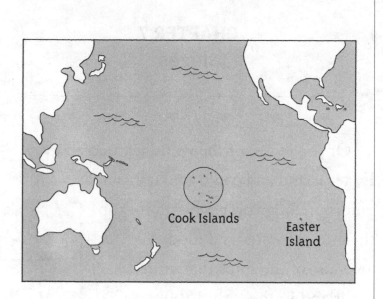

Cook Islands

Easter
Island

adored him. They thought he was almost like a god.
But on his last visit, Captain Cook squabbled with the
Hawaiians. To end the fight, he tried to kidnap the
Hawaiian king. In the heat of the moment, a crowd
of Hawaiians attacked and killed Cook. But then they
gave him an important funeral. They honored him as
if he were one of their chiefs. Eventually, his bones
were returned to the ship's crew, and he was buried
at sea.

CHAPTER 7
Slaves

Once the rest of the world learned about Easter Island and could find it on a map, sailors on long voyages began to stop there to get water and food.

Most of the ships that visited the island in the early 1800s were whaling ships and seal hunters. At first, they were just looking for supplies. They took away fresh water, bananas, sweet potatoes, and yams. Each time, they left behind more disease.

Then in 1805, a ship called the *Nancy* arrived from America. Its captain was a brutal man named J. Crocker. He and his crew attacked the islanders and captured more than twenty of them. He took the islanders onto his ship—as slaves!

A whaling ship

Both the men and the women were kept chained up in the hold of the ship until it had sailed two hundred miles away. Then Crocker let the prisoners come back up onto the deck. He planned to force the prisoners to work for him, catching seals.

But instantly, the Easter Island men jumped into the water and started to swim back home! They didn't realize how far away Easter Island was. Most likely, all the men drowned. (The women were kept aboard the ship and remained slaves.)

Captain Crocker visited Easter Island again, to kidnap more slaves. After that, the island people no longer trusted visitors. Whenever a ship came near, they threw stones at it.

Unfortunately, that didn't stop the whaling ships from coming to Easter Island—and taking more slaves.

In 1862, more ships arrived, looking for slave laborers. This time the slave raiders came from South America—from Peru. They tricked the islanders into boarding their ships or took them by force. If the islanders wouldn't go along peacefully, they were shot!

Many slaves landed in Peru. Slavery was illegal there. But the slave raiders had a way to get around the law. They made the islanders sign a contract, agreeing to work as servants or laborers in the fields of Peru. Some of them were forced into a disgusting job. They had to scoop up huge piles of bird poop from an island offshore, where hundreds of birds lived. The bird poop was called guano. It was sold as fertilizer.

Nearly fifteen hundred Easter Islanders were enslaved in a short period of time. That was more than half the population of the whole island!

Pretty soon, other countries of the world heard about the slave trade. Many thought it was wrong—especially France. French Catholic missionaries arrived in the Pacific islands. Missionaries are people who want to teach their religion to others. The French priests argued against keeping islanders as slaves. A French bishop complained about slavery to high officials in Peru. In Rome even the head of the Catholic Church became involved.

Pope Pius IX

Finally, in 1863, Peru let the islanders go. But freedom came too late for most of them. Many had already died from smallpox in Peru. Others died on the way home. Only about a dozen Easter Islanders made it back to their life on the island.

Slavery

Slavery has existed all over the world for thousands of years, and still exists in some places today. In ancient times, people were captured and

held as slaves in Egypt, China, Greece, and Rome. In Mexico in the years between AD 750 and 800, slaves were used to build huge temples out of stone. In the Middle Ages, local people were held as slaves in England, Spain, and Poland. In the seventeenth century, slaves were brought to North America from West Africa to work on plantations (large farms) in the South. Some worked as servants in the North.

But in the late 1700s, countries began to abolish slavery—to make it illegal. France was one of the first countries to abolish slavery, in 1794. By the 1860s, countries all over the world were rejecting the hateful practice. Slavery was finally abolished in the United States in 1865 after the Civil War ended.

CHAPTER 8
Kings and Birdmen

The French missionaries had done a wonderful thing—helping to free the Easter Island slaves. But not all the French visitors to Easter Island were so kind.

In 1867, a Frenchman named Jean-Baptiste Dutrou-Bornier arrived on Easter Island. He

tried to trick the islanders into coming with him to Tahiti to work for free. When that didn't work, he purchased land from the islanders—lots of land. (The islanders didn't know it supposedly belonged to Spain—

Jean-Baptiste Dutrou-Bornier

and, in any case, Spanish explorers had never returned.) Soon the Frenchman owned nearly all of the island. Most of the islanders moved into one small area near the water, called Hanga Roa. Hanga Roa was becoming the only town on Easter Island.

Then Dutrou-Bornier began to set up a sheep farm. He brought four thousand sheep to the island, along with hundreds of pigs. He also brought horses and cattle. He planned to use the whole island as a sheep farm.

Dutrou-Bornier forced an island woman to marry him. He claimed she was a Rapa Nui queen—so he was a king. He used violence to keep the islanders under his control.

Finally, the islanders rebelled against the cruel "king" and killed him.

But by 1877, there were only 110 people living on Easter Island. Life as the islanders had known it was nearly stamped out.

In the next few years, more misery arrived from the outside world. First, in 1888, the country of Chile decided to claim Easter Island as its own.

Then, eight years later, a Chilean businessman and sheep farmer named Merlet signed a lease for almost the entire island. He forced the islanders to build walls all over the island and told them to "keep out." Then he made them build a nine-foot wall around Hanga Roa. He forced them to stay inside the town. They weren't allowed to leave except to work on his sheep farm. They were prisoners.

The sheep farm did about as much damage to Easter Island as the rats had done. The sheep ate all the native plants. They killed the few remaining trees by eating the bark.

By the time Katherine Routledge arrived in 1914, the sheep ranchers were in total control. The islanders were miserable. They weren't fed well or treated well. Some of them had a terrible disease called leprosy. The lepers were forced to live by themselves outside the town, so no one else would get sick.

But Katherine Routledge went to the leper colony. She was willing to risk it. She wanted to talk to the oldest men on the island—the ones who remembered stories from the past. They were her best chance to learn about the ancient island customs, since none of the stories had been written down anywhere.

The Birdman Contest

One of the stories the old men told Katherine Routledge was about the Birdman contest. It was a game the islanders played in the fall. The winner would be the Birdman, treated like a chief for the year. The goal was to be the first man to steal an egg from a bird's nest high on a very steep cliff on another island. Then he had to bring it back to Easter Island without breaking it.

Finally, the islanders had had enough of the misery. An old woman named Angata walked up to the sheep farm manager's house. She had become a very religious Catholic. She told the manager she had had a dream. In the dream, the manager was gone and the islanders were in charge again. Angata said that God told her people to go outside the walls of Hanga Roa and take some cattle for a feast.

Angata

Angata's son and some other men did just that. They got on their horses and rode off to steal cattle. A fog rolled in from the sea, which made it impossible for the manager to see them leaving. Otherwise, he might have shot them. That night, they had a huge feast.

After that, Polynesians began killing cattle, just to make a point. They wanted the sheep ranchers gone. The islanders fought with the ranchers and the few remaining European visitors.

Even Katherine Routledge was afraid for her own life. She knew the islanders were starting a war—but it was a good war, in her mind. It was a war to regain their independence.

In the end, though, the Rapa Nui islanders didn't win. Officers from Chile arrived by ship. No one was punished, but the islanders were told they could not rule over their own island. Chile would be in charge from now on.

Still, Katherine's visit to Easter Island marked the beginning of a happy change for the native people. For the first time, a European visitor

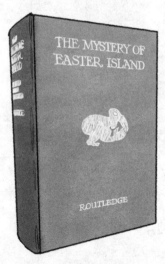

who came to the island did something good for the local people. Katherine wrote a book about the people and the magnificent statues they had carved. It was called *The Mystery of Easter Island*. Instead of sickness and misery, she brought the attention of the world to Easter Island—and enormous respect for their amazing achievements in stone.

But it would be a long time before the Rapa Nui people were once again in charge of their own island.

CHAPTER 9
The Island Changes

Little by little, the island became more like the modern world. The Chilean navy set up a telegraph station on the island so that news could reach the island quickly. In the 1930s, more missionaries arrived. Houses and a church were built in Hanga Roa. Once a year, a ship would arrive with supplies.

The sheep ranchers stayed on Easter Island until 1953. Then the Chilean government finally kicked them off.

Not long after Katherine Routledge's book was published, other scientists began to study Easter Island. Thor Heyerdahl's arrival in 1955 was the most important event for the country in the twentieth century. He brought more attention to the island than anyone else had. Thor was already famous around the world for his *Kon-Tiki* adventure. When he arrived on Easter Island, nearly nine hundred islanders greeted him on the shore.

A member of Thor's crew wrote that the people of Easter Island were openhearted, friendly, and "happy all the time." Even through years of being treated like prisoners and slaves, they had stayed true to themselves and their own kindhearted nature.

By the 1960s and 1970s, Easter Island was well known to the outside world. An airport was built on Rapa Nui in 1965. It was partly used by the United States—as a place to land spy planes that were watching the French conduct nuclear tests. The island became involved in US space missions. In the 1980s, the airstrip was lengthened so it could be used by the NASA Space Shuttle as an emergency landing strip.

The airport also allowed tourists to come to Easter Island. Tourism became the most important business for people living on the island.

In 1966, the Rapa Nui became full citizens of Chile. After that, they at least had a vote in how their island was governed.

Today, Hanga Roa is a modern city, with cars, hotels, and restaurants. About 3,300 people live there. The islanders still live a very simple life, though. Sometimes the electricity goes off or the stores run out of food. But the people are proud of their history and eager to show visitors what a beautiful place the island is.

In 1995, the Rapa Nui National Park on Easter Island was named a World Heritage Site—a valuable place the world should treasure and protect. UNESCO, which is the United Nations Educational, Scientific and Cultural Organization, selects these sites. Other World Heritage Sites include the Giza pyramids in Egypt, the Statue of Liberty in New York City, and the Grand Canyon in the western United States. It's against the law to damage a World Heritage Site.

More than half of Easter Island is a national park now. Thousands of people visit each year. They come to see the moai—the statues—that were once toppled and are now standing again. Little by little, the statues have been restored by archaeologists from the University of Chile. In the 1990s, a Japanese company donated money and a crane to help lift up fifteen fallen statues.

Those fifteen moai are now the ones most photographed. They stand up to five stories tall, in a row on a huge platform near the sea.

Total Eclipse of the Sun

In 2010, tourists came to Easter Island for another amazing sight. On July 11, there was a total eclipse of the sun. An eclipse is what happens when the moon passes between the earth and the sun, blocking the sun out. For almost five minutes in the daytime, the sky went completely dark. It was the first time in 1,400 years that a total eclipse had happened in that part of the South Pacific. Four thousand people came to Easter Island to see it.

Today, about fifty statues are standing, but many more are still scattered across the island. Nearly half of the nine hundred moai on Easter Island are still at the quarry where they were carved, waiting to "walk" to their final destinations. The largest one, still unfinished, is estimated to stand sixty-nine feet tall and weigh 270 tons!

Looking at those giant moai, it's hard not to wonder—what more would the Rapa Nui people have created, if Europeans had never arrived? Would they have built bigger and more beautiful statues? We'll never know. But the world can be grateful for so many giant statues, resting peacefully on the grass or standing proudly at the ocean. They remind us of the peaceful and proud Rapa Nui people who carved them so many years ago.

Timeline of Easter Island

AD 800 –1200	Polynesians come by canoe and settle the island
1722	Jacob Roggeveen becomes the first European to discover the island
1770	Spanish explorers arrive, spreading more disease and claiming the island for Spain
1770s	War breaks out among the islanders
1774	Captain Cook sails to the island
1805	Captain J. Crocker takes away some of the islanders in chains
1862	Slave raiders arrive and take captive islanders to Peru to work
1868	Dutrou-Bornier sets up a sheep farm on most of the island
1888	Chile claims the island as part of its territory
1896	The islanders are kept prisoner by a sheep farmer
1914	Katherine Routledge comes to study the moai
1953	The Chilean government removes the sheep ranchers
1966	The islanders become full citizens of Chile
1986	Pavel Pavel tests his theory about how statues were moved
1995	Easter Island's national park becomes a World Heritage Site
2010	Four thousand people visit the island to watch a solar eclipse
2012	Terry Hunt makes a video of a replica moai "walking"

Timeline of the World

1271 —	Marco Polo leaves on his travels to China
1757 —	John Campbell invents the sextant, enabling sailors to measure latitude
1778 —	Captain James Cook explores Hawaii
1810 —	Chile gains its independence from Spain
1858 —	First transatlantic telegraph cable is completed
1877 —	Edward Very invents the flare gun for sending distress flares at sea
1918 —	Worldwide influenza epidemic strikes, killing nearly twenty million by 1920
1927 —	First vaccine is announced for tuberculosis
1937 —	Amelia Earhart's plane is lost somewhere in the Pacific
1953 —	Edmund Hillary and Tensing Norgay climb Mount Everest
1960 —	Most powerful earthquake ever recorded hits Chile
1970 —	Thor Heyerdahl sails the papyrus boat *Ra II* from Morocco to Barbados
1980 —	Smallpox eradicated
1999 —	First nonstop balloon flight around world completed in twenty days
2012 —	Space probe Voyager I passes beyond the solar system and into interstellar space

Bibliography

Dangerfield, Whitney. "The Mystery of Easter Island." *Smithsonian*,
    March 31, 2007. http://www.smithsonianmag.com/people-
    places/the-mystery-of-easter-island=151285298.

"Easter Island." History.com. http://www.history.com/topics/
    easter-island.

Fischer, Steven Roger. *Island at the End of the World: The
    Turbulent History of Easter Island*. London: Reaktion Books
    Ltd., 2005.

Hunt, Terry, and Carl Lipo. *The Statues That Walked: Unraveling
    the Mystery of Easter Island*. Berkeley, CA: Counterpoint,
    2012.

Hunt, Terry, and Carl Lipo. "Easter Island moai 'walked.'" *Nature*.
    YouTube video. October 23, 2012. https://www.youtube.com/
    watch?v=yvvES47OdmY.

Routledge, Katherine. *The Mystery of Easter Island*. London:
    Watson and Viney, 1919.